In the simmer dim

Barbara Cumbers

*To Helen
from Barbara*

© Barbara Cumbers

First Edition 2022

Barbara Cumbers has asserted her authorship and given permission to
Dempsey & Windle for these poems to be published here.

All rights reserved. No part of this publication may be reproduced, stored in
a retrieval system or transmitted in any form or by any means without the
written consent of the author, nor otherwise circulated in any form of
binding or cover other than that in which it is published and without a
similar condition being imposed on a subsequent purchaser.

Cover photograph: Shirley Markham

Published by Dempsey & Windle

15 Rosetrees
Guildford
Surrey
GU1 2HS
UK
01483 571164
dempseyandwindle.com

A catalogue record for this book is available from the British Library

British Library Cataloguing-in-Publication Data

ISBN: 978-1-913329-75-4

Printed and bound in the UK

Barbara Cumbers

Barbara Cumbers lives in London.

Now retired, she earned her living as an information officer in the NHS and as a part-time lecturer in geology.

She has had poems published in various magazines and small press anthologies. Her first collection, *A gap in the rain*, was published by Indigo Dreams in 2016.

In November 2017 she had a month's residency in Scalloway, Shetland. These poems are a result of that residency, and of several visits to the islands as a geologist.

Her website is barbaracumbers.wixsite.com/barbara

Contents

North	7
Island voices	8
In the simmer dim	9
Hermaness	10
Keen of Hamar	11
Da mirrie dancers	12
Looking for Hendersons	13
Wild geese	14
Grind o da Navir	15
Clearance	16
Bridges	17
Utility	18
Concrete angel	19
A landscape for Sue	20
Burrafirth	21
Beorgs of Uyea, Ronas Hill	22
Treasure Island	23
Yell	24
An eccentric geologist describes the ophiolite fragment that forms the eastern side of Unst and Fetlar	25
Directions	26
Storm petrels, Mousa	27
Harp song to a bonxie chick	28
The road to Melby	29
The Booth	30
Burning	31
Long-tailed duck?	32
Triangular square dance	33
Loch of Funzie	34
The sea as abstract expressionist	35
Gannets	36

Winter puffins	37
Thirteen ways of looking at a bonxie	38
Wick of Skaw	41
Last day	42
South	43
Notes	44

*

Acknowledgements

Thanks are due to Jane Duran, Mimi Khalvati, the Thursday group, and various members of Open University Poets, for their encouragement and helpful comments on some of these poems.

Two of the poems included here have been previously published:

'North' is in *A Gap in the Rain*, by Barbara Cumbers.
    Indigo Dreams, 2016, ISBN 978-1-910834-01-5

'Keen of Hamar' was published in *Envoi*, issue 176, June 2017

North

There is so much light, the midnight sky
is full of it. Not stars nor moon – just light,
the simmer dim enough to read by.
I am drinking light and space. At my back,
the solid rock, metamorphic, ancient,
the grey-red rootedness of Unst. In front
is north, the open sea and the sky shining.

How can I breathe in all this emptiness?
It is clear and warm tonight as air flows north,
rushing away over the far horizon.
The rock at my back grows sharp.
It whispers in the red-gold glow
that the price of summer light is ice,
its thin stone blue, and the deep winter dark.

Island voices

I am the pony on the high moor
the barrel pony of children's dreams.
I am the peat beneath its hoofs.

I wake to the steep of water
that has nowhere to go.
I reach down to ancient carbon

stored in the land. The wind
blows through and around me,
electricity and alien blades

anchored in rock, brown and raw.
I am the islands and the true horizon
of unbroken sea.

I am the orca and also the seal,
the torn and the tearer
of muscle, fur and bone.

I am the hut on the harbour wall,
my facing blue-painted,
my windows shuttered.

In the simmer dim

The sky is hanging loose and huge
tethered lightly to the hilltops —
a breath of wind could blow it away.

Darkness does not fall here, it seeps
from the ground, flows into hollows,
adds form to the shapes between rocks,

a crouching beast perhaps, or an opening
to a space without footholds
where memory purls like a peat-brown burn

touching rocks and grass in passing,
flashes of detail swept round
in the eddies of pools, the falls

over boulders as it catches a twig
to spin and blur. If I try to hold it,
it spills through my fingers.

Hermaness

When you know there's nothing
north but sea and ice,

that the rocks you can see
are the last fixed points,

the squelch of bog feels firmer,
the endless wind less chill,

and the glow in the sky
is all the light you need.

Keen of Hamar

not enough to green
shattered serpentinite
plants are small and scarce
northern rock cress   fragrant orchid   fairy flax

you need to crouch down
and creep forward slowly
eyes close to the ground
dwarf scurvy grass   Norwegian sandwort   spring squill

chromium and nickel
discolour flowers that bloom
purple-tinted
black spleenwort   frog orchid   hoary whitlow grass

they root unnoticed
long fibres finding water
deep below broken stone
mountain everlasting   Shetland mouse-ear   moonwort

Da mirrie dancers

Because the night is shining green
        it might split open

so I wait in the still and the cold
                for the solar wind
        to blow the sky apart

                and sheets of light
to spiral down and swing

            through air with the sound
                of a knife brushing ice.

The voice is distant, bloodless
        like the hiss of iron filings

            as they sing
    to a moving magnet.

There should be no sound,
        I know there can be no sound

yet I hear it
    resonate through
the bones of my skull

        the magnetic bones of my skull
a tinnitus outside myself

            the voice of the north
calling the southerner I am

            to the thinness of dark
that only the north knows.

Looking for Hendersons
for Graham

These forbears are not mine, their roots
are deep in peat — row after row
of Halcrows, Goudies, Taits and Mouats,
some Duncans and Youngclauses,
a walled enclosure of Bruces dating back

and back and back. What Hendersons there are
are recent — James who died in 1977,
Thomasina, his wife, in 1990, Gilbert in 2000
and Jackie 2010. When I ask a lady
tending flowers where older Hendersons might be,

I'm told that they weren't Sandwick folk
but came from down south,
from Scousburgh and Longfield.
From the map, I find "down south"
is six or seven miles away.

On the beach beyond the graveyard
dunlins are running along the shoreline
back and forth as they have always done
while a single turnstone, winter visitor,
worries at rocks and weed.

Wild geese

Just when the sky's ice blue
soars clear of cloud or contrails,

just when a page of light spreads
unwritten from horizon to horizon,

klaxon voices herald
a trailing pennon of geese

taking turns to lead
through the slipstream of air,

a slow pulse of wings
freeing the light's song.

Grind o da Navir

I need the sea for its edges, for its separation
of islands, for its nearness wherever I stand.
Like old age, it teaches me frailty.

This is Eshaness and nothing west
till Greenland. No betweenland here,
no littoral, no soft breathing

in and out of the tide — the tide is up or down,
sea against cliff. Rock shudders higher
or lower, but still shudders.

I walk out in wind, easy walking
grassland with its many ladder stiles
to this broken ridge — two tonne blocks,

rectilinear as if cut by machine.
The sea has considered
a new career as quarryman, its dynamite

exploding rocks to send them far inland.
I look around and under boulders
like a seal woman searching for her skin.

Clearance

People carry all they own, desperation
on their faces, the future invisible
in the hollowness of now. Less bloody
than war but no less brutal

is their clearance from the land,
surplus population of an island
now for sheep, inferior beings
whose worth was measured in profit

and found wanting. The coast
of the only land they know
grows fainter. They feel the deck
move beneath them, hear gulls crying.

Bridges

Without hustle or rush the few who lived here
farmed or fished, small boats plying the straits
and open sea. Leaving was by ferry

that chugged its way to Scalloway, where
a bus would drive on narrow winding roads
to Lerwick, slow and slow and slow.

Now there are bridges built from oil
that let a thousand people get to town and back
in half an hour. In the white of the bridge

low over water, a single track of tarmac marks
where Mainland ends and Trondra begins,
island folk travelling faster, now coming back.

Utility

This little bay's a perfect arc of sand
tide-smoothed, holding no footprints but my own.
Above the sand there's weed, above that stones
storm-driven upwards, adding to the land.
Naked bones lie there — a long-dead seal,
intact, with rags of skin still softly furred
and clinging to ribs. All flesh has gone, no blur
of flies now clouds the open body. Small
and thorough scavengers have rasped it clean
as men would once have done — blubber, skin
and meat all utilised. Bones were ground
to lime what little soil there was. And now
an empty carcass stripped by snails and birds
is left here for a storm tide to disperse.

Concrete angel

The vision of an angel
had to be carved, to be carved
in stone where no blocks of stone
were large enough

or fine enough for the vision,
so the sculptor cast his own
as he cast ideas onto paper
and carved them in stone,

in stone for all to read,
to read and to question,
to question the loss, the loss
of balance in the waste,

the almost unnoticed waste
as a small local brightness
guttered away downslope
and into the harbour.

A landscape for Sue
Keen of Hamar, Unst, Shetland

I want to give you a landscape
like no other, that you will likely
never see, for the plantsman in you.

It is Mars in its bareness,
a dry expanse of broken stone
beneath an enormous sky.

Clouds move in from the west
with frequent rain that drains
quickly away. There are

no trees, no mountains,
though there are cliffs, and always
the sound of wind and sea.

You would cross a ladder stile
from a cattle link of grasses
lush with dung onto bare serpentinite

to find plants that live only here.
They have unromantic names like
Edmondston's chickweed, and are tiny

in air, though their roots stretch
down and down to the water they need
that the surface cannot hold.

Burrafirth

I love to be early
when dew is still
shining like frost
when only my trail
shows green through
whitened grass
I love to walk
westward and see
my long shadow
climb the hill
ahead of me
as the bog blips
in growing warmth
and overhangs
of sphagnum drip
into dark pools
and to know that
soft vapours rising
cloud my feet alone

Beorgs of Uyea, Ronas Hill

A place of boulders and shadows,
no houses, no trees, no roads,
what paths there are are ill-defined,

the stuff of the hill revealed
in left-overs of ice and the scatterings
of axe factories, flakes shaped

with stone on stone from felsite dykes
that cross the granophyre
by folk who have left us little but this

where now is only ourselves
and granophyre and fragments of felsite
in the sound of wind and emptiness.

Treasure Island

It came to him here, the outline
ready beneath his feet. Of course
Flint's island must be Caribbean,

isolated; it must have forest
where wild pigs or goats
could thrive; but Unst

would be its shape — inlets,
caves and hills, somewhere
for Jim to beach *Hispaniola,*

safe anchorage behind an islet.
From Muckle Flugga
and his father's lighthouse

south to Uyea, from Saxa Vord
to Gallow Hill — the geography
he needed rooted in the sea.

He could put the treasure
anywhere — it was already here
in the peat of the island,

its crofts and chromium
and northernness, its serpentinite,
all the contorted rock of it.

Yell

The gateway to the northern isles
is not a destination. The road-makers
knew the way of it — avoid the coast

and any habitation, skirt all villages,
send the cars from Ulsta to Gutcher,
from ferry to ferry, as fast as you can,

set blinkers round drivers' eyes
so all they see is tarmac, peat and sky
on their way to somewhere else.

An eccentric geologist describes the ophiolite fragment that forms the eastern side of Unst and Fetlar

Snake-rock, too old to remember the ocean floor,
lies on its side under too-shallow sea and incongruous air.

Snake-rock has lost the twisty knots it's named for,
left us clibber and mystery.

Snake-rock is heavy with metals prohibiting peat.
It grows small discoloured plants.

Snake-rock does not know the names we call it by —
dunite, harzburgite, gabbro — ochre, grey, and black.

If snake-rock could dream, its dreams would be
of weight and time, of scrape and crush.

Oh, the stress in flattened pebbles.
Snake-rock has secrets locked away, written in water

it holds as part of itself. In layers of settlement,
snake-rock carries the stripes of its past.

Directions

not north or south   south
is safe   and north

is nowhere   maybe up
higher than the hills

where lines   retreat
round the curve of the earth

or it could be   out to sea
mirage of land   lost

in the troughs of waves
rootedness   displaced

by the ever-tilting line
of the horizon

instead   there is inward
the wanderings

along the borders of sleep
dark crossings

guarded   the warmth
of your body   not here

Storm petrels, Mousa

A tiny smut of darkness
                separates from sea

      flutters   merges
with the black of the broch

             then another   more
     until our eyes fill

with fleeting specks
             as if we'd stared
     too long at brightness

or a bonfire
     out at sea
             were scattering ash

             dark urgent motes
     flitting landward

             intermittent beings
of a summer night

Harp song to a bonxie chick

Hatched on Unst's far northern fastness
you've not yet seen a night of darkness
only a dip in daylight's vastness.

You've not yet flown past cliffs of granite,
hunted puffins, stalled a gannet
unfazed you're smaller, lighter than it.

You're crouching, fearful, now in heather
yet when grey down's replaced by feather
you'll rule the air in any weather.

And when the signs of summer slacken,
when west gales blow and night skies blacken
the south will call you — it's life's pattern.

Though most who visit here defame you,
the summer folk can hardly blame you —
they'll fly south too when tropics claim you.

But, fluffy chick, this island bred you,
cliff and moor, the sea that fed you —
it's home wherever winds have sped you.

The road to Melby

Past cnoc and lochan, cnoc and lochan,
        the road weaves

                and the air is sparking.
        Tarmac hardly wider than the car

                rises and falls like the other road
in the middle distance

whose direction masks
        that it is the same road draped

round cnoc and lochan, cnoc and lochan,
        a thread of grey sewn through the heather.

                White markers of passing places
        catch the light.

Cnoc and lochan and light,
        a landscape not lit, but of the light,

                folds of it clothing the land
into part of itself.

The Booth

Wood boarded walls are painted blue,
red shutters frame the windows —
it's a dolls' house on the harbour wall.

Unhook the front, open it and see
a woman inside alone,
keeping house as if it were real,

sharing with wind and waves
truths she did not know she knew
in that huge absence.

Burning

The sea is aflame across the harbour
and all the way to the horizon.
And through the fire

a black ship's hull is shimmering,
a distant processionless Up-Helly-Aa
or a funeral taking the dead to sea

to meet Viking gods of ice and fire
who live here still in the peat
and the salt wind.

In truth it's a sunset
flaming the base of clouds
and the tops of waves,

the burning ship is the fishing boat
I saw leave with its crew of three,
yellow waterproofs bright with wetness,

technology keeping it safe.
The harbour reflects its red
up through my window

and wavelight dances on the ceiling.
The ship is burnt
on my retinas white-on-green.

Long-tailed duck?

I argue with myself about a duck,
small, white and alone.
A flock of eiders swimming close
ignores it, some shags, a seal. The duck
dives down with partly open wings,
flying into water, flicking its tail
upwards. The air's so still today
it hardly feels like Shetland.
The wind will be back tomorrow
and I will argue with myself again
about I know not what.
I think this is a long-tailed duck
Clangula hyemalis, though its tail
is short and it's not quite like
the pictures in my book.
I check the web — so many
varied photos, various moults
— and there it is, a duck
like the one by my window,
small, white and alone.

Triangular square dance

Three large birds, one black, one black and white, one brown
stand equidistant round a boulder. On the boulder lies a rabbit,
freshly dead. The birds eye the meal in the rabbit
and they eye each other. Nothing moves except the wind
shuffling grass blades, ruffling feathers. No music starts the dance.

Raven croaks, hops forward, wings half opened, huge.
Black-backed gull cries its raucous loudness. Raven stops, retreats.
Bonxie makes a leap toward the boulder, then back
as Gull and Raven turn. Three large birds around a boulder
give each other space, and wait. Gull's turn to rise.

The others join it, dancing a looping air dance over rabbit.
Three feathers, one black, one white, one brown
drift down to land on rabbit. Three large birds
land equidistant round a boulder, places changed.
Then it's Raven's turn again and another round begins.

Loch of Funzie

You'd think it was a toy, a rubber duck
small-headed, spinning, swimming
far too buoyantly as if to catch the wind

to take it anywhere. This rarity
is what I'd hoped to see, the rain
supplanted by a red-necked phalarope,

a tiny bird that chooses here to breed
and nowhere else, finding this small loch
on this small island again and again.

The sea as abstract expressionist

streaks of bright blue rope
        frayed ends splayed

highlight of a yellow buoy

        tattered orange net spread
            over shredded plastic

fractured lettering
        on battered boxes

            rhythmic assemblage
       of jetsam

       beach-strewn
from careless open ocean

        shells and shingle
            here and there

            incongruous
       intrusive nature

Gannets

They fill the air round coated cliffs lightened
in guano by their ancestors, enhanced
each generation as they add the whiteness
of themselves. Their size is dwarfed by distance,
two metre ink-tipped wings, easy flights
above the waves in silence. Only here
at nests they call — guttural cries that might
have come from Viking throats, the roar of sheer
numbers of partners greeting, changing places
as one flies off to fish, a lazy glide
then upward, almost clumsy as it scales
the air, its shoulders hunched until it steadies,
folds itself, becomes a spear, and dives,
a javelin thrown between the sky and sea.

Winter puffins

They have lost the comic noses
worn all summer, taken them off
and thrown them away; bright lines

accentuating eyes have gone, their garb
now unremarkable — drab and monochrome.
No longer do they walk their waddling walks

on large red feet over rock and grass
where, if they had canes to twirl, they surely
would have twirled them; no longer

do sand-eel false moustaches waggle
as they duck and scurry into burrows.
They have gone to sea. The cliffs are bleak.

Thirteen ways of looking at a bonxie
(after Wallace Stevens)

1.
Deep in their dark
bruised eyes
bonxies see
that pugnacity
needs no cause.

2.
The sea and the wind
are one.
The sea and the wind and the bonxie
are one.

3.
I know jealousy and theft
and the trustless guarding
of what I call mine;
and I know too
that the bonxie is a part
of what I know.

4.
There are good things in the world
that the bonxie knows
are there for the taking.

5.
In the long darkness
where no bonxies are
the sea calls their name.

6.
Like draughtsmen
awaiting a game,
bonxies array themselves
on the moor.

7.
Oh, oil men of Sullom,
why do you imagine gentle birds?
Do you not see how the bonxie
extorts what it can?

8.
The bonxie inhabits
enormous skies;
an enormity of being
inhabits the bonxie.

9.
Two brothers saw a mermaid
and fought each other for her favours
until they both died;
bonxie shadows fall on their land.

10.
Geologists' bright helmets
protect their heads
from falling rocks
and low flying bonxies.

11.
In its fluffiness
the bonxie chick
knows nothing
of piracy.

12.
Which do I prefer?
The endless wind
and treelessness
of the island, or
the ocean floor of it?
The bonxie
or its absence?

13.
Morning and evening twilight
spread towards midday;
bonxies fly south
low over the water.

Wick of Skaw

Small waves break, trap air, and boom on sand,
a drum more loud than such a wave should beat
on such a shore where rusting labelled baskets

shield rare plants, and no-one comes. A sunny
summer Sunday and only I am here.
No deck chairs, coloured windbreaks, ice-cream stalls,

no shops for knick-knacks, no-one playing ball;
only a beach, low cliffs and fallen boulders
of a xenolithic porphyritic granite.

Some terns are hovering, light and whitely elegant
beyond the drumming waves. Four gannets cross
the wick, white crosses ink-tipped, effortless.

Last day

An otter surfaced near me quite by chance.
I needed a piss and crouched beside a wall
sheltered from the wind. A lucky glance —
a whiskered face emerging from a pool.

I needed a piss and crouched beside a wall
below the skyline, clothes in disarray.
A whiskered face emerging from a pool
dripped with water only yards away.

Below the skyline, clothes in disarray,
I played at statues, watched the otter draw
itself from water only yards away.
I'd never seen a wild one close before.

I played at statues, watched the otter draw
its body to a circle, clean its fur.
I'd never seen a wild one close before.
At ease in its environment, it turned

its body to a circle, cleaned its fur.
A cold and muddy walk, a northern bay's
not my environment, it's time I turned
southwards, towards home. On my last day

a cold and muddy walk — a northern bay
sheltered from the wind. A lucky glance
southwards towards home on my last day
lit on an otter near me quite by chance.

South

Narrow track to the road, car bumping on ruts,
splashes of mud. Slowly, slowly.

I could be driving to the shop.
I could need milk, or butter, or bread.

Not vegetables — they come from the smallholding
where I've dropped off the key to the croft.

Pause at tarmac, let a lorry go by,
pull out, turn south, over the brow of the hill

down into town. Slow past the ferry terminal
where *Hrossey*'s moored, empty of passengers,

filling with freight at this time of day,
a busyness of cleaners, mechanics and seamen

checking and checking and checking.
Hrossey's not taking me anywhere.

Almost turn in at the Co-op, then on
past bus station, shops, houses,

up the hill at Sound and onto the moor.
Drive on south and further south,

Quarff, Fladdabister, Cunningsburgh, Sandwick.
I can still pretend it's a normal day —

I'm on my way to the lighthouse or Jarlshof,
or could be. Pretend and keep pretending

until I don't drive past the airport.
This is it. There's my plane.

Notes

p9 *Simmer dim*: the Shetland name for the absence of darkness in midsummer.
Unst: the most northerly inhabited island in Shetland.

p11: *Keen of Hamar*: a botanical nature reserve on Unst, Shetland.

p12: *Da mirrie dancers*: the Shetland name for the Northern Lights

p15: *Grind o da Navir* ("gap of the borer" in Shetland dialect) is a cleft high up in the sea cliffs of Eshaness which funnels storm waves with such force that huge boulders are carried a couple of hundred metres inland.

p17: Trondra and West Burra were linked to each other and to Mainland in Shetland by bridges built in the 1970s with money from the oil industry. The population of the islands increased markedly.

p19: A concrete angel was cast and carved in about 1919 by William Johnson, stonemason of Scalloway. It was broken up late 20th century and used as hard core for a harbour jetty extension. Johnson had eccentric ideas about gravity which he published in a book called "The law of universal balance". He engraved a summary of his ideas into a cornerstone of his house in Scalloway that can still be read today.

p 22: *Granophyre*: a pink rock similar to granite but finer grained. *Felsite*: a very hard, fine grained volcanic rock from which prehistoric people in Shetland made stone tools.

p23: R L Stevenson visited Unst in 1869, ten years after his father and uncle had built Muckle Flugga lighthouse off its northern coast. *Treasure Island* was published in 1883, with a map that bears a superficial resemblance to Unst.

p24: Yell, the second largest island in Shetland, is described as "the gateway to the northern isles" in its tourist brochure.

p 25: *Ophiolite*: a piece of ocean floor now on land. The name is derived from the Greek for snake rock.
Clibber: the Shetland name for a type of soapstone much used by the Vikings for carving into bowls and cups.

p28: *Bonxie*: the Shetland name for the great skua, a highly aggressive sea bird about the size of a herring gull. Large numbers of them breed in Shetland.

p29: *Cnocs*: small rounded hills usually separated by shallow lakes.

p30: *The Booth:* a well-equipped hut beside the harbour at Scalloway, Shetland, where artists can spend a month on creative projects.

p31: *Up-Helly-Aa*: The Shetland fire festival held in January that includes the burning of a full-size replica Viking long ship.

p41: *Xenolithic*: a crystalline rock containing enclaves of a different composition.
Porphrytic: a crystalline rock containing very large crystals within a finer groundmass.
Wick of Skaw: the most northerly beach in the British Isles, on Unst.